APOSTOLIC LETTER

OF HIS HOLINESS

POPE JOHN PAUL II

ON THE OCCASION

OF THE FIFTIETH ANNIVERSARY

OF THE OUTBREAK

OF THE SECOND WORLD WAR

VATICAN CITY

CONTENTS

I. Apostolic Letter

On the Occasion of the Fiftieth Anniversary
of the Outbreak of the Second World War / 3

The hour of darkness / 3
To remember / 5
The action of the Holy See / 6
Man treated with contempt / 8
The persecution of the Jews / 9
The trials of the Catholic Church / 10
Totalitarianism and religion / 12
Respecting the Rights of Peoples / 13
Disarmament / 14
Educating Younger Generations / 15
Bringing Moral Awareness to Public Life / 16
An Appeal to Europe / 17
A Word to Catholics / 18

II. Appendix

Message of His Holiness Pope John Paul II
to the Polish Episcopal Conference / 21

To my Brothers in the Episcopate,
To Priests and to Religious Communities,
To the Sons and Daughters of the Church,
To those in Government,
To all people of good will,
Health and the Apostolic Blessing.

The hour of darkness

1. "YOU HAVE LAID ME IN THE DEPTHS of the tomb, in places that are dark, in the depths" (*Ps* 88/87:7). How many times this cry of suffering arose from the hearts of millions of men and women who, from 1 September 1939 to the end of the summer of 1945, were confronted with one of the most destructive and inhuman tragedies of our history!

While Europe was still in shock over the power tactics employed by the Reich in annexing Austria, breaking up Czechoslovakia and conquering Albania, on 1 September 1939 Poland was invaded by German troops from the West, and on 17 September by the Red Army from the East. The crushing of the Polish army and the martyrdom of a whole people was unfortunately only a prelude to the fate in store for many European peoples as well as for many others over most of the five continents.

From 1940 onwards, the Germans occupied Norway, Denmark, Holland, Belgium and half of France. During this time the Soviet Union, already enlarged by a part of Poland, annexed Estonia, Latvia and Lithuania, and took Bessarabia from Rumania as well as certain territories from Finland.

Furthermore, like a fire spreading destruction in its wake, *the war and the human tragedies* that accompanied it inexorably and rapidly *expanded beyond the borders of the "old continent" and became a "world" war.* On one front, Germany and Italy carried the fighting beyond the Balkans and into North Africa; on another, the Reich suddenly invaded Russia. Finally, by destroying Pearl Harbor the Japanese brought the United States of America into the war on the side of England. This was the situation at the end of 1941.

It was necessary to wait until 1943—with the success of the Russian counteroffensive that freed Stalingrad from the grip of Germany—for a turning point in the history of the war. The Allied Forces on the one hand, and the Soviet troops on the other, succeeded in crushing Germany at the cost of fierce fighting, which from Egypt to Moscow inflicted unspeakable suffering upon millions of defenceless civilians. On 8 May 1945 Germany offered her unconditional surrender.

The struggle in the Pacific, however, continued. In order to hasten the end, two atomic bombs were dropped on the Japanese cities of Hiroshima and Nagasaki at the beginning of August, 1945. Following that appalling event, Japan in turn capitulated. It was 10 August 1945.

No war ever merited the name "world war" in the way that this one did. *It was also a total war,* because in addition to land operations there was air combat, as well as naval combat on all the world's oceans. Whole cities were mercilessly destroyed, and their terrorized populations reduced to anguish and misery. Rome itself was threatened. The intervention of Pope Pius XII prevented the city from becoming a battleground.

This is a sober summary of the events which we remember today. They caused *the death of fifty-five million people, left the victors divided and Europe in need of rebuilding.*

To remember

2.   Fifty years later, *it is our duty before God to remember* these tragic events in order to honour the dead and to share in the sorrow of all those whom this outbreak of cruelty wounded in body and soul, while at the same time forgiving the offences that were committed.

In my pastoral solicitude for the whole Church, and with concern for the good of all humanity, I could not let this anniversary pass by without inviting my brothers in the episcopate, priests and laity, and all people of good will to reflect on the process which brought this conflict to the very depths of inhumanity and suffering.

This is because we have *the duty to learn from the past* so that never again will there arise a set of factors capable of triggering a similar conflagration.

We now know from experience that the arbitrary dividing up of nations, the forced displacement of peoples, rearmament without limits, the uncontrolled use of sophisticated weapons, the violation of the fundamental rights of individuals and peoples, the non-observance of international rules of conduct and the imposition of totalitarian ideologies can lead to nothing but the ruin of mankind.

The action of the Holy See

3.   Pope Pius XII, from the beginning of his pontificate on 2 March 1939, did not fail to issue *an appeal for that peace* which everyone agreed was seriously threatened. A few days before the outbreak of hostilities, on 24 August 1939, he spoke prophetic words that still resound today: "Once again a grave hour is at hand for the whole human family... The peril is imminent, but there is still time. Nothing is lost with peace. Everything can be lost with war".[1]

Unfortunately the warning of this great Pontiff was not heeded and disaster struck.

[1] Radio Message, 24 August 1939: *AAS* 31 (1939), p. 334.

The Holy See, unable to prevent war, tried to *stop it from spreading* by using its limited means. The Pope and his advisors made relentless efforts to this end, both on the diplomatic level and in the humanitarian field, without letting themselves be drawn into taking sides in a conflict which pitted peoples of different ideologies and religions against one another. In this task they were also preoccupied not to aggravate the situation or to compromise the safety of peoples subjected to extraordinary trials. With regard to what was happening in Poland, Pius XII declared: "We ought to speak words of fire against such things, and the only thing that dissuades us from doing so is the knowledge that if we should speak, we would be making the condition of these unfortunate ones more difficult".[2]

A few months after the Yalta Conference (4-11 February 1945), and with the war in Europe barely over, this same Pope, addressing the College of Cardinals on 2 June 1945, did not fail to *look to the world's future and to plead for the triumph of law:* "Nations, especially those that are small or moderate-sized, demand that they be permitted to control their own destinies. They can be led to accept, of their own free will and in the interest of common progress, obligations which modify their sovereign rights. But after having borne their

[2] *Actes et Documents du Saint-Siège relatifs à la seconde guerre mondiale,* Libreria Editrice Vaticana, 1970, vol. 1, p. 455.

share —their large share—of sacrifices in order to destroy a system of brutal violence, they are right in refusing to have imposed upon them a new political or cultural system which the great majority of their peoples resolutely reject... In the depths of their conscience, people feel that their leaders would discredit themselves if, caught up in the mad frenzy of the hegemony of power, they failed to bring about a triumph of law".[3]

Man treated with contempt

4. This "triumph of law" remains the best guarantee of respect for persons. In returning to the history of those six terrible years, it is only right that one regard with horror *the contempt in which man was held.*

To the *material ruins,* to the annihilation of the agricultural and industrial resources of countries ravaged by fighting and destruction, including the nuclear holocaust of two Japanese cities, one must also add *massacres and misery.*

My thoughts turn in particular to the cruel fate inflicted on the peoples of the great plains of Eastern Europe. At the side of the Archbishop of Krakow, Adam Stefan Sapieha, I personally witnessed this distressing reality. The inhuman demands of the occupier of the moment brutally oppressed opponents and suspected opponents,

[3] *AAS* 37 (1945), p. 146.

while women, children and the elderly were subjected to constant humiliation.

One can never forget the tragedy that resulted from the *forced displacement* of peoples who were thrown onto the roads of Europe, exposed to every peril in their search for a refuge and for the means to live.

Special mention must also be made of the *prisoners of war,* who in isolation, destitution and humiliation paid yet another heavy price after the harshness of battle.

Finally, one must remember that the creation of *governments imposed* by the occupier on the States of Central and Eastern Europe was accompanied by repressive measures and even by numerous executions in order to subjugate the resistant peoples.

The persecution of the Jews

5.   Among all these anti-human measures, however, there is one which will forever remain a shame for humanity: *the planned barbarism which was unleashed against the Jewish people.*

As the object of the "final solution" devised by an erroneous ideology, the Jews were subjected to deprivations and brutalities that are almost indescribable.   Persecuted at first through measures designed to harass and discriminate, they were ultimately to die by the millions in extermination camps.

9

The Jews of Poland, more than others, lived this immense suffering: the images of the Warsaw ghetto under siege, as well as what we have come to learn about the camps at Auschwitz, Majdanek and Treblinka, surpass in horror anything that can be humanly imagined.

One must also remember that this murderous madness was directed against many other groups whose crime was to be "different" or to have rebelled against the tyranny of the occupier.

On the occasion of this sorrowful anniversary, once again I issue an appeal to all people, inviting them to overcome their prejudices and to *combat every form of racism* by agreeing to recognize the fundamental dignity and the goodness that dwell within every human being, and to be ever more conscious that they belong to a single human family, willed and gathered together by God.

I wish to repeat here in the strongest possible way that hostility and hatred against Judaism are in complete contradiction to the Christian vision of human dignity.

The trials of the Catholic Church

6.   The new paganism and the systems related to it were certainly directed against the Jews, but they were likewise aimed at Christianity, whose teaching had shaped the

10

soul of Europe. In the people of whose race "according to the flesh, is the Christ" (*Rom* 9:5), the Gospel message of the equal dignity of all God's children was being held up to ridicule.

In his Encyclical "Mit brennender Sorge", my predecessor Pope Pius XI clearly stated: "He who takes race, or the people or the State, or the form of Government, the bearers of the power of the State, or other fundamental elements of human society ... and makes them the ultimate norm of all, even of religious values, and deifies them with an idolatrous worship, perverts and falsifies the order of things created and commanded by God".[4]

This pretension on the part of the ideology of the National Socialist system did not spare the Churches, in particular the Catholic Church, which before and during the conflict *experienced her own "passion"*. Her fate was certainly no better in the lands where the Marxist ideology of dialectical materialism was imposed.

We must give thanks to God, however, for the many witnesses, known and unknown, who in those hours of tribulation had the courage to profess their faith steadfastly, who knew how to rise above the atheist's arbitrariness and who did not give in to force.

---

[4] 14 March 1937: *AAS* 29 (1937), p. 149 and p. 171.

7. Nazi paganism and Marxist dogma are both basically *totalitarian ideologies,* and *tend to become substitute religions.*

Long before 1939, there appeared within certain sectors of European culture a desire to erase God and his image from man's horizon. It began by indoctrinating children along these lines, from their earliest years.

Experience has unhappily shown that once man is abandoned to human power alone and crippled in his religious aspirations, he is quickly reduced to a number or an object. Moreover, no age of humanity has escaped the risk of man closing in upon himself in an attitude of proud self-sufficiency. But such a risk is accentuated in this century insofar as armed force, science and technology have given contemporary man the illusion of becoming the sole master of nature and history. This is the specious claim that lies at the root of the excesses we deplore.

The moral abyss into which contempt for God and thus for man plunged the world fifty years ago made us touch with our very fingers, as it were, the power of "the ruler of this world" (*Jn* 14:30), who can seduce consciences through falsehood, through *scorn for man and for law,* and through *the cult of power and force.*

Today we remember all these things and meditate on the extremes to which the abandonment of all reference to God and to all transcendent moral law can lead.

8.   What is true for the individual is also true for peoples. In recalling the events of 1939 we are reminded that the cause of the last world conflict was the crushing of the rights of whole peoples as much as those of individuals. I recalled this fact yesterday, in my letter to the Polish Episcopal Conference.

There can be no peace if the rights of all peoples—particularly the most vulnerable—*are not respected!* The entire edifice of international law rests upon the principle of equal respect for States, for each people's right to self-determination and for their free cooperation in view of the higher common good of humanity.

It is essential there never again occur situations like that of Poland in 1939, in which a country was ravaged and divided up at the pleasure of unscrupulous invaders. In this regard, one can hardly help but think of those countries which have not yet obtained their full independence, as well as those which face the threat of losing it. In this context and in these days, we must call to mind the case of Lebanon, where united forces, pursuing their own interests, have not hesitated to imperil the very existence of a nation.

Let us not forget that the United Nations Organization was born after the Second World War as an instrument of dialogue and of peace, based upon *the recognition of the equal rights of peoples.*

13

Disarmament

9.   One of the essential conditions for "living together" is disarmament.

The terrible trials undergone by both combattants and civilian populations at the time of the Second World War must move the leaders of nations to make every effort at hastening the development of a *process of cooperation, control and disarmament* which will make war unthinkable. Who would dare still justify the use of horrendous weapons which kill people and destroy the work of their hands in order to resolve differences between States? As I once stated: "War is in itself irrational and... the ethical principle of the peaceful settlement of conflicts is the only way worthy of man".[5]

For this reason, we must give a favourable reception to the negotiations now taking place for nuclear and conventional disarmament, as well as those aimed at a total ban on chemical and other weapons. The Holy See has repeatedly declared that the parties involved must at least arrive at the lowest armament level possible, commensurate with the demands of their security and defence.

These promising developments, however, will only have a chance to bear fruit if they are supported and accompanied by the will to intensify *cooperation equally in other areas, notably in the areas of economics and culture.* The last

[5] *Message for World Day of Peace,* 8 December 1983, n. 4: *AAS* 76 (1984), p. 295.

meeting of the Conference on Security and Cooperation in Europe, held recently in Paris on the theme "The Human Dimension", expressed a desire by the countries of both parts of Europe to see *established everywhere the rule of the State governed by law.* This form of State would appear, in fact, to be the best guarantor of the rights of the individual, including the right to religious freedom, respect for which is indispensable for social and international peace.

Educating Younger Generations

10.   Having learnt from the mistakes and moral failures of the past, Europeans today have a duty to pass on to younger generations a lifestyle and culture inspired by *solidarity with others and esteem for them.* In this regard, Christian faith, which has so deeply moulded this continent's spiritual values, ought to be a source of constant inspiration. Its doctrine of *the person created in the image of God* can only contribute to the thrust towards a renewed humanity.

In the social debate which is inevitable whenever different conceptions of society meet, adults must give an example of respect for others, always being able to recognize the part of the truth which the other person possesses.

On a continent with such marked contrasts, we must continually learn anew *to accept one another,* as individuals, as ethnic groups and as countries, with all our differing cultures, beliefs and social systems.

Educators and the media have a fundamental role to play in this regard. Unfortunately, it must be said that education in the dignity of the person created in the image of God is certainly not favoured by the portrayals of violence and depravity which the social communications' media all too often disseminate. Young consciences in the process of formation are troubled by these, and the moral sense of adults is dulled.

Bringing Moral Awareness to Public Life

11. *The fact is that public life cannot bypass ethical criteria.* Peace is achieved first of all on the terrain of human values, values that are lived and transmitted by citizens and by peoples. Whenever the moral fibre of a nation begins to wear away, the worst is to be feared.

Vigilant remembrance of the past ought to make our contemporaries attentive to potential abuses in exercising the freedom which the war generation sacrificed so much to attain. The fragile balance of peace could easily be compromised if evils such as racial hatred, contempt for foreigners, segregation of the sick and the elderly, exclusion of the poor, recourse to private and collective violence were revived in people's consciences.

It is the responsibility of citizens to distinguish, among various political proposals, those

16

that are inspired by reason and moral values. It falls to States to be vigilant in halting anything that would lead to exasperation or impatience on the part of any disadvantaged group within society.

An Appeal to Europe

12.   To you, statesmen and leaders of nations, I repeat once again my profound conviction that *respect for God and respect for man go hand in hand.* They make up the absolute principle which allows States and political blocs to overcome their hostilities.

In particular, we cannot forget Europe, where this terrible conflict first sprang up, and which experienced a genuine "passion" which left it ruined and drained of its life's blood. Since 1945 we have been witnesses to and active participants in praiseworthy efforts aimed at the material and spiritual rebuilding of Europe.

Yesterday, this continent exported war. Today, its role is to be a "peacemaker". I am confident that the message of humanism and liberation, which is the heritage of Europe's Christian history, will once again energize its people and continue to shine forth in the world.

Yes, Europe, all eyes are upon you, because people are aware that you still have something to say after the catastrophe of those years of fire: namely, that *true civilization is not*

17

to be found in force, but rather is *the fruit of a victory over ourselves, over the powers of injustice, selfishness and hatred* which can go so far as to disfigure man himself!

A Word to Catholics

13.   In conclusion, I wish to address in a special way the pastors and faithful of the Catholic Church.

We have just recalled one of the bloodiest wars in history, a war which broke out on a continent with a Christian tradition.

Acknowledgement of this fact compels us to make *an examination of conscience* about the quality of Europe's evangelization.   The collapse of Christian values that led to yesterday's moral failures must make us vigilant as to the way the Gospel is proclaimed and lived out today.

Unfortunately, we must observe that in many areas of existence modern man thinks, lives and acts as if God did not even exist.   In this, we find lurking the same danger that was present yesterday: that man will be handed over to the power of man.

While Europe prepares to put on a new face, while positive developments are happening in certain places in its central and eastern parts, and the leaders of nations collaborate to an ever greater degree in solving the great problems of humanity, God is calling his

Church to make her own *contribution to the coming of a more fraternal world.*

Together with other Christian Churches, and despite our imperfect unity, we wish to say once again to humanity today that man is only authentically himself when he accepts that he is a creature of God; that man is only aware of his dignity when he recognizes in himself and in others the imprint of the God in whose image he was created; that man only achieves greatness to the extent that he makes his life a response to God's love and puts himself at the service of his brothers and sisters.

God does not despair of man. As Christians, neither may we despair of man, for we know that he is always greater than his mistakes and his faults.

Recalling the Beatitude once spoken by the Lord, "Blessed are the peacemakers" (*Mt* 5:9), we wish *to invite all people to pardon each other and to put themselves at each other's service,* for the sake of him who, in his flesh, "put an end to hostility" once and for all (*Eph* 2:16).

It is to Mary, the Queen of Peace, that I entrust all mankind, confiding to her maternal intercession this history in which we all have a part to play.

In order that the world may never again know the inhumanity and barbarism which ravaged it fifty years ago, let us tirelessly proclaim "our Lord Jesus Christ, through whom we have now received our reconciliation" (*Rom* 5:11). It is Christ who is the pledge of our own reconciliation with each other!

May Christ's Peace and Blessing be with all of you!

From the Vatican, 27 August 1989, the eleventh year of my Pontificate.

Joannes Paulus II

MESSAGE

OF HIS HOLINESS

POPE JOHN PAUL II

TO THE

POLISH EPISCOPAL CONFERENCE

ON THE OCCASION

OF THE FIFTIETH ANNIVERSARY

OF THE OUTBREAK OF WORLD WAR II

1 SEPTEMBER 1939

1.   "AND NOW WE COME to the most important point of our message", said Pope Paul VI on 4 October 1965, in addressing the General Assembly of the United Nations Organization: "You are expecting us to utter this sentence, and we are well aware of its gravity and solemnity: *not some peoples against others,* never again, never more!   ... Many words are not needed to proclaim this loftiest aim of your institution.   It suffices to remember that the blood of millions of men, that numberless and unheard of sufferings, useless slaughter and frightful ruin, are the sanction of the past which unites you with an oath which must change the future history of the world: *No more war, war never again!* Peace, it is peace which must guide the destinies of peoples and of all mankind " (*AAS* 57, 1965, 881).

2.   The first of September 1989 is the fiftieth anniversary of the outbreak of the Second World War.   When the western border of Poland was attacked in the early morning hours of that day, all her people were quick to respond to the armed invasion, and did not shrink from war in defence of their mortally threatened homeland.

Little more than twenty years had passed since Poland had regained her independence and had been able to begin anew a life of self-determination as a sovereign State. Although during that relatively brief period she had encountered many difficulties, both from within and from without, she had nonetheless experienced real progress on the way to her development. Consequently, the will to defend the homeland was clear and decisive, even though the embattled forces were unequal. The unparalleled effort in defence of the homeland and its essential values, an effort mounted by the entire society and particularly by the younger generation of Poles, was worthy of admiration and lasting remembrance.

This determination to defend the independence of the State accompanied the sons and daughters of our Nation not only in the occupied country, but throughout the world, wherever Poles struggled for their own freedom and that of others. Indeed, *the war,* which began on the first of September, soon spread to other countries in Europe and abroad. Other peoples became victims of Hitler's invasion, or found themselves exposed to a dire threat. Very soon it was recognized that the war demanded a defence of Europe and its civilization against totalitarian aggression. Throughout the war, the *Polish people fulfilled completely,* even extravagantly, *its obligations as an ally* and paid the highest price for "our liberty and yours".

24

Even Poland's losses bear witness to this fact. They were immense, perhaps much greater than the losses of *any other Allied country*. *Above all, there was loss of life, coupled with an enormous devastation of the country,* in both its western and its eastern territories. As we know, on 17 September 1939 Poland was also invaded from its eastern border. The non-aggression pacts which had been signed earlier were violated and cancelled by the Accord of 23 August 1939 between the German Reich and the Soviet Union. That Accord, which has been described as "the Fourth Partition of Poland", was also the death sentence for the Baltic countries which bordered Poland on the North.

It is truly difficult to calculate the magnitude of the losses suffered, and even more, of the *sufferings which were inflicted upon individuals,* families and communities. Many facts are already known; many more must yet be brought to light. The war was waged not only on the front, but as a *total war,* a war which struck entire societies. Whole groups were deported. Thousands became victims of prison, torture and execution. Quite apart from strict combat, people died as victims of bombing and of systematic terror. The organized instruments of the latter were the *concentration camps,* ostensibly established for labour, yet transformed in reality into *death-camps.* One particular crime of the Second World War remains the massive extermination of the Jews, who were doomed to the gas chambers because of racial hatred.

When all of this passes before our eyes, the words of Pope Paul VI to the Assembly of the United Nations take on their full significance. The historical reality of the Second World War is indeed even more terrible than any terms that might ever be used to describe it.

3. *But do we need to speak about it?* Fifty years after its outbreak, the generation which experienced the war and its sufferings is still living. But at least two generations have grown up since the war, generations for whom the war is only a chapter in the history books. We need to ensure that that tragic event never cease to serve as a warning.

The United Nations Organization showed that it recognized this fact when, immediately after the conclusion of the war, it published the *Charter of Human Rights.* The eloquence of that document is fundamental. The Second World War made all people aware of the magnitude, previously unknown, which contempt for man and the violation of human rights could reach. It led to an unprecedented marshalling of hatred, which in turn trampled on man and on everything that is human, all in the name of an imperialistic ideology.

Many people were led to ask *whether,* after that terrible *experience, it would ever be possible to have any certainty again.* After all, the horrors of the war had taken place on a continent which could claim a remarkable flowering of culture and civilization—the continent which had remained so long in the light of the Gospel and the Church.

In reality, *it is not easy* to press forward and to leave behind *this terrible Calvary endured by individuals and nations.* Only one point of reference is left, and that is the Cross of Christ on Golgotha, of which Saint Paul says: "Where sin increased, grace abounded all the more" (*Rom* 5:20). Guided by this faith, the Church, together with the men and women of our century, with the peoples of Europe and of the entire world, *seeks to chart a course towards the future.*

4. The search for this new "course" involves all those who live on the continent of Europe. In a special way, it involves Poland, which, fifty years ago, was the first to attempt to say a decisive "no" to the armed aggression of Hitler's State, and the first to pay the price for her determination. On all fronts, even in the underground struggles carried on within the homeland, and in the Warsaw Uprising, our Nation's sons and daughters showed in countless ways how much they took to heart *the cause of our country's independence.* But once that terrible struggle was over, they were forced to ask themselves whether the decisions made at the end of the war truly respected the immense contribution made by their efforts and sacrifices. Although they were on the side of the

victors, they were forced to ask themselves whether they were in fact being treated as the vanquished. This sort of questioning became more and more insistent, and impelled them with increasing force to undertake new struggles. For in truth, *a State whose society is not sovereign is no sovereign State at all.* Such is the case when a society has no chance to decide what constitutes the common good, and when it has been denied the basic right to share in power and responsibility.

In outlining the moral principles which ought to have inspired the world after the conclusion of the war, Pope Pius XII forcefully emphasized the fact that "within the limits of a new order founded on moral principles, there is no room for violation of the freedom, integrity and security of other States, no matter what may be their territorial extension or their capacity for defence". Turning then to the realm of economics, the Pope recalled the rights of nations "to safeguard their economic development, since only in this way shall they be able to achieve adequately the common good, and the material and spiritual welfare of their people" (Radio Message, 24 December 1941, *AAS* 34, 1942, 16-17).

It is hard to fight the conviction that the post-war period failed to provide the growth and the progress which the Polish Nation so greatly desired and needed, given the devastation of the Second World War. Rather, the period in question provoked *a great so-*

cio-economic crisis and new losses—losses no longer suffered on the fronts of armed conflict, but on the peace-time front of the struggle to build a better future for the homeland, and the struggle to ensure a rightful place for it among the nations and States of Europe and of the world.

5.   I wish to return once again to the words of Paul VI. I referred to these words twice during my visits to Poland (2 June 1979 and 17 June 1983). I repeat them once again in the present context. Pope Paul stated that: "*A Poland that is prosperous and serene... is also beneficial for the tranquillity and good collaboration of the peoples of Europe*".

These words were addressed to Poles, and it surely depends upon Poles themselves, to a decisive decree, whether Poland will in fact be "prosperous and serene"; whether she will be a country of progress on many fronts; whether she will make up for the slackening pace (not merely confined to the economy) which is the bitter fruit of the system which has exercised power; whether she will be able to restore among her millions of citizens, particularly her youth, a confidence in her own future. All this depends on Poles themselves.

Pope Paul VI's words were also addressed to *all of Europe: both East and West.* No one can erase the record of responsibility for actions which have weighed down so terribly upon the history of our nation and that of the other nations of Europe.

The mutual decision of August 1939—the Accord signed by the representatives of the German Reich and the Soviet Union which condemned Poland and other countries to death—was no unprecedented event. It was a repetition of a policy which had already been decided at the end of the eighteenth century by our neighbours in both the West and East: a policy which was systematically carried out right up to the beginning of this century. Then, near the middle of our own century, the same *decision of destruction and extermination was repeated.*

The nations of Europe must not forget this. In particular, on this continent, which has been called "the Europe of homelands", they must not forget *the basic rights of both the individual and the nation!*

It is also necessary to build a system of forces such that no superpower, be it economic or military, can ever destroy another country and trample upon its rights.

6. "Will the world ever succeed in changing that selfish and contentious mentality from which so much of its history has been woven?", asked Pope Paul VI in his Discourse to the United Nations Organization. His answer was: "It is not easy to foresee. On the other hand, it is easy to affirm that we must resolutely march *towards a new future, a future of truly human peace,* that peace which God has promised to men of good will" (*AAS* 57, 1965, 882).

30

It could be said that Europe, contrary to appearances, is not yet completely healed of the wounds inflicted throughout the course of the Second World War. For this to happen, tremendous effort and resolute determination are needed both in the East and in the West. A genuine solidarity is needed.

Into the hands of the Polish Episcopal Conference, on the first day of September 1989, I place these hopes and wishes for the future of our homeland.

7. On this day, communities of believers in Europe and throughout the world will gather in prayer. How many people will have to be embraced by that prayer—their sufferings, their generosity, their sacrifices and above all their deaths, all brought back to mind? And there are not only those who endured sufferings and death; there are also those who inflicted them, those who bear an enormous responsibility for the horrors of the war. They will meet God's judgment bearing that responsibility. How many people, how many millions of human beings, must our prayer really embrace on this day?

Can we compare them to that "great multitude" seen by Saint John in the Apocalypse (cf. *Rev* 7:9)? This "vision" of the Apocalypse was not under the law of death and destruction alone. For the "blood of the Lamb" was also present, that Blood which is at work with the power of the Redemption, and is itself greater than any power of destruction and evil which mankind has known upon this earth.

Gathered in prayer on this day which recalls the fiftieth anniversary of the great destruction of the Second World War, let us never cease to reflect anew upon the divinely inspired words: "Behold, I make all things new" (*Rev* 21:5).

With these words Christ reminds every new generation of the truth of his saving Paschal Sacrifice.

I place these thoughts, this prayer and a lively hope into the maternal hands of the Queen of Poland, Our Lady of Jasna Góra, in whom God has given us a "wondrous help and bulwark".

Given in Rome, at St. Peter's, on 26 August, the Solemnity of Our Lady of Czestochowa, in the year 1989, the eleventh of my Pontificate.

Joannes Paulus II